BLISSED AND UNSTOPPABLE

10 THINGS YOU NEED TO KNOW ABOUT BEING BLISSED AND UNSTOPPABLE TODAY

MANISHA SHAH

Published by "The Great Indian Book Tour"
Imprint : Holistic Publishing
www.tgibt.com
106/91, Ashok marg, Vijay path
Mansarover, Jaipur, Rajasthan-302020
Phone : +91-72400-68114
email : prashant@tgibt.com

Title : **Blissed and Unstoppable**
Author : **Manisha Shah**
Copyright © Manisha Shah 2023
All rights reserved

First published in 2023
First Edition 2023
Printed in India

ISBN : 978-93-93262-31-8

Dedicated to Supreme power

GRATITUDE TO MY MENTOR
SANDEEP DHYANI

When there was so much darkness in my world you gave light to it. I feel that a mentor guides us to live a happy life. I am forever grateful to you for all the teachings you have given and still give me. I am blessed to have a mentor like you. Each teaching and time that you have given to me, it's priceless to me. According to me, life teaching is the biggest teaching in the world which no one tries to give. I am blessed to have that from you.

Your teaching played an amazing role in my life. That's why I am blissed and unstoppable today. Words are not enough to describe my gratitude towards you.

At last, I want to say thank you from bottom of my heart and I will always make you feel proud.

ABOUT THE AUTHOR

Manisha Shah is renowned as a Bestselling author, a singer and a teacher. She is a much-loved author of **"THE ONE WHO IS EVERYTHING FOR YOU IN YOUR LIFE"**. Her simple style of narration and the life lessons in her stories deliver a deep message which has the power to transform people's lives.

Blissed and Unstoppable is her second book, intended to bring forth change in people's life. She believes her prosperous words can definitely change someone's life as it has changed her life fully.

Her second book is based on her real-life experiences and the steps she followed once for being blissed and unstoppable.

You can write to her at manishashah482@gmail.com or follow her on Instagram – manishashah4822021

ACKNOWLEDGEMENT

My deepest gratitude to my late grandfather Mr Darshan Singh Shah, who raised my father with great etiquette of life. Being or having a hearing disability never led him to feel down. He was best in his way. The great worker and jewellers learned work from him. I am grateful that I am his granddaughter. I have learned from him that do not let your weakness be the excuse for being excellent at the thing you want in your life. Grandpa, I love you so much and miss you, you will always and forever be alive in our hearts.

My heartfelt gratitude to my late grandmother Mrs Rajeshwari Devi, who was extremely patient, kind, and loving and who taught me to be in discipline. I still remember the way she used to make dishes for us and asked us to be patient to taste them, she never used to allow us to have a bite until everyone is not ready to have a meal. Granny, I love you so much I learned from you, how to be patient, kind, loving, and disciplined. The day you left us I was too small to understand that you will never come back and I thought you were in the hospital that day I was so excited to gift you a heart balloon because you used to love me the most. Grandma, I miss you so much you are alive in my heart forever.

BLISSED AND UNSTOPPABLE

With all my heart I am grateful to my late paternal uncle Mr Surendra Singh Shah who faced a lot of struggle and pain in his life, which he didn't able to bear sometimes and used to hide. He was heartbroken and failed to be the best in his vital roles in life. His wife left him, his children left him. He was not in hope even that he could be the best and make everything best again during unbearable pain he got a heart attack and he left us. I have learned from my Paternal Uncle that something we can't change so that we can do best is to live in the present in which we have control. He used to play ludo with us, he used to recite stories. He used to tell us how to be happy all the time but now I got to know how much pain he suffered. He is not with us but he will be forever in our hearts. I love you Uncle so much. My Paternal Uncle used to be good at writing and I wish he could able to see my writing skill now but I know he will be with us forever.

I am truly grateful to my Father Mr Moti Shah who has achieved success after a lot of hard work and has never denied learning something new. Who always tells me that nobody can copy our pattern of thoughts or our talent, and this thing itself is a masterpiece. He taught me no matter how hard things appear if we smile at it, we feel relaxed, this will give us the courage to try again. His journey from being a tea vendor to a utensils seller led him to find his talent while selling tea he used to listen to songs and thought one day he will be successful like those who shine. He did so much hard work. His story inspires me so much whenever I think about it. He is extremely talented and unbeatable in music. My Father is a famous music director in the Hillywood industry and gave the Hillywood more than a thousand plus songs. People admire him so much. His hard work paid off whenever he gets the award for his best work I feel like I want to be good as he is in his work. I have learned many things from him which are uncountable. The most important which I follow is "Don't try to fit on other's benchmark create your benchmark because records are meant to be broken". I love you so much papa, you are my everything.

My heartfelt gratitude to my Mother Kamla Shah, who is the most loving, caring, kind-hearted woman who taught me to be happy every time and value myself. My Mother is a woman who always tries her best in everything. No doubt she is the most amazing daughter, sister, wife and mother. She always understands everyone. She is the only one who can feel instantly the pain of the person. Her words are like the cure for all problems. Her positive vibes and teachings led me here. She is the only one who used to say "Don't cry over things that didn't happen because you don't know how many best things are waiting for you. Her statements gave me the courage to be the one I am today. Nobody can be like you mummy, you are the best in the whole world. I want to be like you. You are best in everything while giving proper time to the family you worked hard to be the best singer in the hillywood industry. Your voice is incredible, loving, and fabulous. I have learned from you that people are most important than things and I learned to give value to people from you. I love you so much, mummy. You are my inspiration and my everything.

With all my heart I am grateful to my elder Sister Miss Pooja Shah who encouraged me to be the best in everything. She always stands beside me to protect me from all downfall. She taught me that if we would determine the thing we want we would be able to achieve it. She is the pure soul and helping hand to overcome the negativity. She taught me how to write and read in my childhood. She is the one who always used to bring things for me to eat when she used to come back from her school. I love you so much Dii for everything you have done for me. I want to create many more memories and to make our all dreams come true which we used to think about in childhood while sitting on the roof. You are my power and no doubt you are the best versatile singer.

I am truly grateful to my younger Sister Surbhi Shah who is always there to motivate me and to tell me how much best I am. She is the only one who encouraged me and pushed me day and night to make my novel happen. I am forever grateful to you Surbhi for each statement that you said to me before writing the book and being an Author. I doubted myself so much throughout the journey to being an Author. Your excitement towards my writing, wanted me to write more and here I am. I loved the way you obey my every statement without questioning me. I feel really bad about the way I used to deny in front of people that you are my sister to just make you the best in everything without using my identity and you obeyed me as always but in the end, you got my intention for doing all these, so I love you so much suru. I will make your all dreams come true because my biggest dream is to fulfil all your dreams. I am so proud to be your elder sister. Now see I have told the world you are my sister. I wish you would be happy after reading this note.

I am truly grateful to you Tannu and Pushpam. Your excitement towards my writing seriously makes me feel so happy all the time. I still remember during the exam time my debut novel came out and you were super excited to read it during the final exam. You read my book and also became the first reviewer of my book. Thank you so much for your excitement.

With all my heart I am grateful to my all students and readers, your immense appreciation and love always make me feel motivated and energetic toward my writing and teaching profession.

Introduction

So finally you have chosen this book, I want to congratulate you all for being at the starting point of the Blissed and Unstoppable journey. I am so excited to tell you and will guide you on how can you be blissed and unstoppable. Like others, what the difference all people made that's why they are shining today. I am sure you all are curious to know as I had curiosity before to know all these. And this book itself is telling you how much blissed and unstoppable I became by the grace of supreme power.

Choosing this book also is not a simple act it's guidance from your Inner voice, God, Universe, or any Supreme power which you trust unconditionally. I want to thank that Supreme power that somehow I became a part of your life even though we have not met. No matter whether we have met each other or not. I am still grateful to help you out and it is my promise to you all that if you would take each step seriously my mission to make you blissed and unstoppable will be fulfilled. The journey is so simple and yet very interesting to be one of those who are extremely happy and made their dreams into reality.

This book surely helps you to transform your life fully, you will experience on the last page of this book that you would not be the same as earlier. From all aspects, you will be in a different world to experience all the goods of life.

So are you ready to take this roller coaster ride of life with me? But before we begin this journey I want you to put the blindfold on your eyes, and hold my hand with complete trust so that I can lead your way towards the destination that you all wanted to reach for a long time. I promise you I will not let you fall. You are meant to be blissed and unstoppable.

You are here to do which till now nobody has done. You are here to achieve the heights, you are here to experience unlimited abundance, you are here to be the one who you always wanted to be, you are here to be unstoppable because nobody was like you in the past, nobody was like you in the present and there will be nobody in the future also who will be like you.

Accept this fact you are a unique creature created by god, everybody can copy you but nobody can become like you because you are the original copy. You are a blessing on this earth. There is the purpose of your birth to experience all the goods of life. So let me hold your hands to show you the way to have prosperity, abundance, and riches of the whole world. It's never too late to experience anything new. Put a blindfold of trust on your eyes and let me lead you towards your desired destination.

Let's begin the incredible journey together.

Chapter 1
Surrender

Surrender is the first thing to experience for the world you want. Let me give you an example as you surrender your body to your brain so your brain gives all the directions to your body as if you want to walk. Your brain will give direction to your leg to move to the destination where you want to go in a result you have surrendered yourself to the brain and you are following its instructions.

Another example is when you came on earth to experience this world, you were not aware of anything. You didn't know how to talk, walk, and eat all the activities which you are doing today. How did all things happen without your effort just because you had surrendered yourself to your parents a result you know how to do all things properly.

As we grow up we are afraid to surrender, we want to do all things on our own. Imagine the new baby boy born and continuously he is trying to bent, eat, and walk by himself no matter how hard he will try. He will get hurt in the end because till now he hasn't surrendered himself.

Imagine the brain which we haven't yet surrendered, it would fail to give directions to our body. It's bitter truth no matter how hard you try to achieve something if you haven't surrendered yourself to the Supreme power, the name could be anything for you of that power. For Example - Jesus, God, and Universe then there will be no guidance on your way.

Note: - Surrender yourself now to the Supreme power, let the power make the decisions in your life. Be ready to see Unfolding, Gifts, and surprises which Supreme power has for you.

Chapter 2
Fire in desire

There should be a fire in the desire for your dreams because dreams are the projection of your abilities and capabilities. Your dreams are like a movie and its little glimpse projection is the trailer of the movie.

If you know what you want and you have done the first thing "Surrender" it will help you to believe in the movie of your dreams.

Let me share the example with you. We all eat food so for making delicious meals we keep the food more time on heat because cooking requires fire. Same as our dreams or our desires give us a glimpse of the movie, for making it a reality you need fire. Yes, you heard it right.

Fire of insult, heartbreak, bad situations, and problematic circumstances helps us to know our true strength and potential.

You might like gold, and gold ornaments because

it has value, and the value increases once the price gets high.

But for making gold ornament what do jewellers do? They keep the gold in the fire. Until it's not ready to mould or ready to be in the design of the ornament. They keep it in the fire.

So the fire of pain, insult, and heartbreak are giving us heat so that we can mould ourselves to be valuable, to be the best version of our own instead of being in depression or anxiety.

We have to gear up the car to reach our destination.

If you like the movie of your dreams you need fire in your heart to make it a reality.

Example: - Neha Kakkar is a famous singer in India and all over the world. What made her blissed and unstoppable? Her home problems, the insult when people used to say to her that she is not good with her heights. Heartbreak in the bad circumstances of her home where she faced a financial crisis.

She made herself amazing today. She is living her dream life. She is on the top. She is at that height in her career where people will not think about her height of the body.

She ignited the fire in her desire, after all these you know what she is now.

Note: - Ignite the fire in your desire now to live the life of your dreams.

Chapter 3

The noise of the world and the voice of your own

There are many things in life you might want to experience and somehow sometimes you discourage the idea to make it into reality because of the noise of the outer world, where everybody just denies the fact that you can. So they keep telling you to not even think about the thing you want to achieve.

Accept this fact that they are not denying because they have analysed your ability towards the work you want to fulfil. They are denying it because they weren't able to make it or they haven't seen anybody achieve so good in just that age in which you are now.

Their experience forced them to say no to the thing they want to fulfil but it doesn't tell about you at all that how much capable you are to achieve your dreams. So don't let the noise of the outer world allow you to worry or give you Anxiety.

Let me give you the example of Motivational Speaker Sandeep Maheshwari. He has tried things in his life and failed to achieve them. The outer world kept on interrupting him to do photography but it wasn't something he wanted to do. Outer world noises came on his way again and again to distract him but he made a difference when he listened to his voice.

Once you surrender yourself, you have fire in your desire and you will not allow the noise of the outer world to make you feel sad, also you will not accept any other assumptions according to the outer noises about you so you will be blissed and unstoppable like him. As you can see Sandeep Maheshwari owns a company, he is a famous Motivational Speaker and he is helping the world because he listened to his voice that what he wanted in his life and now he is a renowned personality.

Note: - Don't allow the noise of the world to interrupt you from your goal because it's all unworthy of you. Listen to your voice to understand yourself better and your goals.

Chapter 4
Importance of yours

Have you ever thought, what is your importance in someone's life? I know most of the answers will be yes, because the truth is, you are not only the one who thinks in this way. Many people think in the same way but they are the only ones who are most stressed today. They are living a life where they feel so much worry about it. This question always makes them feel sad.

In our life, we all are struggling to get importance in someone else's life because we are the ones who are not giving importance to ourselves.

Nowadays we don't have our "me time". The time when we just be with ourselves and feel the importance of our existence. We don't value ourselves, we don't give importance to ourselves in a result we come across people who don't value us because we are the ones who don't like us and in return we want everybody to give importance and love us unconditionally.

Let me ask you how many times have you taken out the things in which you are not the best.

Many answers will be "Many times". There are people whom I met in my life and you also must have seen somewhere, they keep on taking out the things in which they are not good enough they spend their every second of the day thinking like this.

Example: -

- Their hairs are not good.

- Their face is not clean.

- They have a dark complexion.

- They are too thin or chubby.

- They are not good at Maths.

- They didn't do anything in life just because they are not intelligent enough to understand the content matter.

- They are not tall as others.

Many people think or spend their time on this. Once we think of all points of ourselves in which we are not good, indirectly we are not giving importance to ourselves, we are not giving value to ourselves. We insult ourselves many times when we think like this.

Imagine spending time with a positive attitude and counting the best points about you every second of the day, increasing the importance of yours in your life and then you don't have to ask for the importance which people should give to you.

Thinking in this way will change your whole day's experience, and at the end of the day, you will be happy.

If you think in this way: -

• I am the best at English and I am sure I can be good at Maths also.

• I am the best dancer and I am sure I can be a good singer also.

• I am the best singer and I am sure I can play the instrument also.

OR in another way, you can say: -

• I am chubby but I am so cute.

• I am short in my height but I have a great personality.

• I have a dark complexion but I am so attractive.

We all know Shahrukh Khan. He is a famous Actor all over the world.

When he wanted to be an Actor, he said to his relatives and friends that I want to be an Actor.

Everybody didn't give him the importance and said to him that he can't be an Actor because his face cut is not good and he is not handsome also.

As I told you earlier Noise of the world and a voice of your own. He knew that he can, why did he think that he can be the best Actor? Because he gave importance to himself. He didn't ask for his importance from others but he knew if he will give importance to his existence then the world will give him importance.

As a result, you know in everyone's heart Shahrukh Khan is there. In everyone's life, he made his importance because he was the one who gave importance to his look, style, and everything. He became qualified in his mind that he is the best Actor and handsome star before going to audition.

Note: - Well, giving importance to your own can transform your life fully. Once you count in every second of the day at which thing you are the best at rather than counting the things in which you are not good and if you give assurity to yourself that if I am best in this so I can be best in other things too.

Start giving importance to yourself from now onwards.

Chapter 5
The first step toward your legacy

Have you ever thought to live life and leave the legacy behind?

Your every moment, your everyday which you are living is a footprint of your legacy, once you will understand the importance of yours as I said earlier, you would able to understand your desire. The thing is, many people failed to achieve their desires because they haven't given priority to them.

Road of Riches is necessary to take priority towards your dreams and it makes you determined to be good as much as you can and that particular thing helps you to create your legacy.

So living life in a way in which people will admire you after you would have gone. Your life after you, your life moment after you can create a lot of differences in people's life. Everybody on the earth wants to do something big and unique but they are finding the uniqueness outside that's why they are not able to give something unique to the world. Uniqueness is inside of you. You can observe it through your pattern of thoughts and the way you see life but due to a lack of recognition of your uniqueness every time, you fail to achieve your desire.

Understand this "you are a blessing in this whole Universe". Give "me time" to yourself to find the real you, your values, your flaws, and your best thing that all things can make a lot of difference in your life and it will also help you to create your legacy.

You haven't decided now because you haven't given priority enough to your dreams. If you would not initiate the process so, how all things will come up? Your first thing is the priority that you need to give to your dreams.

Example: - You have been thinking to learn driving for 30 years. You haven't made it till now just because you didn't give priority, there was not a single second when you thought to start it now. Every time you procrastinated because you don't want to go through the experience of it, you just want to be perfect at driving.

But, have you ever thought that without taking out single step outside of your house you would be able to reach your destination?

So the priority is important and stepping in towards the first thing can automatically lead your way because you have already surrendered yourself to Supreme power.

Example: - Mahatma Gandhi is a famous patriotic leader, as an Indian we all know what he has done for our country. The life we are living today, he has a big hand in it. Who was he? A normal man who knows laws. He saw farmers living the life which they shouldn't live. He became a helping hand and from then he used his whole knowledge to give us a Freedom and happy life too. He just took a simple first step which led him to be renowned and now everyone knows him. Even in our Indian currency, we have a picture of Mahatma Gandhi.

That was the first step towards his legacy when he agreed to help farmers.

What happened later, its history.

Note: - When you start something for your biggest desire when you give priority to it when you initiate the process for your dream life, you make the first footprint towards your legacy and when you achieve your desire you create a legacy.

So are you ready to take the first step towards your legacy now?

Chapter 6
Healing is the true happiness

The only way to get permanent blissful and happy life is to get healed first. There are many things we need to acknowledge about ourselves if we truly want to heal ourselves.

Healing helps you to overcome your fear, pain, depression and insult. Everyone wants to feel relaxed and want to get healed from all the bad things that had happened to them and just because of all those things.

Just as comparison, jealousy, hate, competition, grudges, gossip and negative things come into their life. For being happy we need to remove all those things from our life and accept the fact. Now you must be wondering, what's the fact?

Let me tell you.

If somebody has insulted you and gave you pain which you hadn't expected from them and somewhere it's still hurting you deep down, it means you didn't heal your heart wound yet and it is still fresh now as well as present in your heart till now.

Once you will heal your heart from all the bad things then you will feel deep inside that you are all set to experience happiness.

The true happiness you can feel if you will heal yourself with three simple steps.

1. **Forgiveness:** - You must have heard the statements many times those who forgive know how to value things, relationships, everything, and for creating a legacy you have to value everything. Forgiveness helps you to heal your wound. Just think if someone has done something bad to you that you didn't like so just forgive them. Forgive them just not for it that they deserve your attitude of forgiveness, forgive them because you want your inner peace.

Suppose somebody said you can't do anything in your life and this statement hurt you so badly, why because you took the meaning out of it. That yes, I can't do anything in my life.

Simply in our day-to-day life, we listen to many voices like fans, machines, and vehicle sounds. We don't pay attention to it, we don't give it any meaning because it's not what we want to listen so we pretend to not listen even though some people don't focus this much as well so they don't care. They only listen to voices which they want to listen and they consider other things as noises.

If you connect the listening example with this meaning example so you would be able to understand what I want to say so just forgive them, not for them but for you. Let them go from your heart don't hold them. They have already filtered themselves from your life but you are the one who is holding all the things.

2. **Pay gratitude:** - Pay gratitude to all people who have given you a lot of suffering and pain. Just because of them you can find a new you, your strength, your power, your capabilities, your abilities just because of them you are living a life where you are thinking to do something big in your life or want to do something big. The way they gave you pain and did all unexpected things to you made you capable to be here where you are now. This thing only leads you where you want to reach. Say thanks to each one of them from your heart. They gave you strength. They helped you to find the real you, the unique you. Don't hold grudges against them just say thanks, and pay gratitude to all of them.

Example: - Akshay Kumar is the famous Bollywood Actor. When he was poor he wanted to click the picture with a good background so he chose to stand in front of the beautiful bungalow to click the picture. Suddenly security guard burst on him with bad words that he can't afford the bungalow and that it's not allowed to click the picture in front of that bungalow. He paid gratitude to the guard. Why? Because his words hit him so badly somewhere he took his words seriously and became capable to live in the same bungalow.

So actually those people who hurt us help us to find our realness, our uniqueness, without them it wouldn't have been possible for you to be here. Think in this way and pay gratitude to them from bottom of your heart. They lit the fire inside you to be the best.

3. **Count good things about people who hurt you:** - Counting good things about them who hurt you so badly can help you feel better. Once you see their positive sides they wouldn't hurt you that much because you are the only one who allowed them to be with you as badly as they can. If somebody has said something or done something unexpectedly bad it means those people know you better. People who know about you more can hurt you more. So if they know you so you also must have known them. Be the pure soul, a good soul, and patiently count the good things about them as much as you can until you feel light from your heart.

Note: -

1. Don't compare or compete with someone just to be better than them. You are unique in your way,

you are a unique creature created by god.

2.   Don't hate or be jealous of people just because they are doing well in life, they are getting what they deserve.

3.   Don't steal somebody else's place to shine, create your place.

Don't have grudges, don't gossips, and don't say negative things about anyone. Make yourself pure. Treat people the way you want to be get treated by them.

Chapter 7
Glad game

A glad game is an activity in which you have to count the things for which you are glad.

Example: -

1. I am glad that I have an android phone.

2. I am glad that I am living in my own home.

3. I am glad that I am perfect with my health.

4. I am glad that I can pay all the expenses of my daily needs.

5. I am glad that I have everything which once I desired to have.

This glad game helps you to find the things about which you can feel glad such as Health, Wealth, Career and Relationships. In these topics of life, you can count the things for which you feel glad in your life.

When we feel stressed out or sad, we focus on what we don't have which takes us towards a negative energy world but this glad game will help you to feel the infinite positive energy. For playing this activity, you don't require any special time or any objects like a pen or paper. You can do this at any time with any activity you do daily.

Example: - Suppose that you are preparing dinner and for cooking food you need to do so many steps before putting things on a gas stove. During the whole cooking process, you can play this glad game in your mind or you can say it out loud. It will make you feel so good.

In your childhood, you must have played many games but this game seriously will help you to experience the tears of joy in your eyes and after some seconds you might forget your all worries and you will be at ease to feel joyful and blissful life ahead.

Think if you would do this activity three times a day how much happier you will feel. As it's written in history, wherever we focus it expands. If we focus on glad things it will expand and if we would focus on bad things it will expand.

Don't play the blame game, just play the glad game to experience the life you want to live.

Note: - Play this glad game now to bring forth the happiness in your life to be blissed and unstoppable like others.

Chapter 8
Appreciate others

Appreciating is the first step towards spreading positive vibes and love. Love makes things easy for us to understand if you love something you must not forget to appreciate it out loud. When we don't appreciate we feel jealous, frustrate and inside our hearts we compare we feel unworthy.

How all sorts of things happen just because of what we like instead of appreciating on the spot we keep it in our heart which stops the love to flow, stops the positive vibes to flow.

Our all appreciation words can make someone's day and create a positive aura around us. Suppose you like someone's beauty, without thinking twice go to the person and say you are so beautiful I like your beauty I admire it.

This will bring gods riches towards you because you have indicated supreme power that you love beauty like her, as a result, you will observe the quality of the things you appreciated by heart coming into your life. It can be a car, mobile phone, beauty etc.

All day if you will make your habit to find appreciating things around you then your all focus will be on the good things and it will help you to be in a joyful mood 24 hours a day. This will make your way easy towards a blissed and unstoppable journey.

Those who know how to appreciate others, and love things are blissed and unstoppable, those who always complain they are not blissed and unstoppable because all day they are bringing hatred and negativity which they don't want in their life.

Today if you step outside or look outside from your home, you have to see things and appreciate them in your mind or you can say them out loud.

Example: -

1. Wow I like this car, I love the colour of this car.

2. I love that girl's hair, I want to have the same hair as her.

3. I love these shoes it suits well on her dress up.

4. I love the glow on her face I want the glow on my face like hers.

In these statements you appreciated just what you loved, you didn't question why I didn't have this or why except me everyone has this. You just shared what you love so you spread love and positivity.

Those who are crippling and comparing always remain unsuccessful. They are never able to feel or give love to nature that why they are never able to have all the love that nature has for them. They try to see negativity in every good thing.

Example: -

1. Oh! This car, the car is nice but who has given this car to him?

2. Yes, the girl's hair is nice but will she be able to take care? I don't think it will last forever like this.

3. Yes, the colour of the shoes is nice but the quality is not that good.

In these statements, we are loving other things but instead of appreciating, we are finding fault. We are spreading negativity. You don't have to wonder how it all happened. How did a person achieve this? If you loved it so appreciates it without thinking twice. Don't pretend that you don't like it.

Those who love to do back-biting, those who are jealous and envy someone else's success and those who compare, they always remain unhappy and un-successful. They can't able to feel blissed on their way ahead in their life.

Appreciating others helps us to bring positivity

to life.

Note: - Start appreciating everything you love which is around you and spread love as much as you can.

Chapter 9
Acceptance

Do you know how good it feels when you get to know there is no problem in your life?

People want to live a happy lifestyle, they don't want to get worried about little - little things but what are the things which are still there deep down inside our hearts? Let me simply explain to you.

The solution to all problems is to accept people as they are, yes it's very easy to say and difficult to obey my words but as you promised me that you will follow my words.

In our life we meet people, we get attached to them and we try to change them as we want them to be.

Soon people get irritated, a fight happens and frustration begins. Yes, there are times that we need to change things which we don't like but forcing some-body to change is not good until that person doesn't feel in himself or herself to change because change is necessary when things are not good enough.

Rather than changing someone accept them as they are and if you don't like something about them, say that you might be right on your way but I am a bit disappointed by this.

Clarifying the point matters a lot, thinking bad about people and having hatred for them is not good.

If you let people be as they are, most of the problems will resolve. Just like if you don't like the way a person behaves with you so might be there other things good about him/her that's why you are with them so let them be as they are.

If you keep on pressurising yourself just because of someone whose company you don't like so instead of being with them just choose to exit that person's life.

If you love the person so accept him/her as the person he/she is. A beautiful bond begins to flourish with the quality of acceptance.

Example: - Everyone's life story is different, they are performing different characters, they are facing different challenges their past actions experienced contributed them to be who they are today. They all are right in their way instead of judging them set them free.

Don't question their wings if they can fly or not

because everyone has the choice to live their life in their way. There is no right and no wrong.

Note: - Nourish the bond of every relationship by "acceptance". Eliminate the negativity and thoughts of judgement. Everyone is perfect in their way. Give them love as much as you can.

Chapter 10
Best version of you

Everybody wants to be successful in life without knowing that they can create success for themselves.

Satisfaction of mind is a success. To show society that we can be good in our work is a successful life for people

The real meaning of success is to know your worthiness. You may want to be a millionaire but what if you are the only one feeling inside how can it be possible? Because somewhere in your mind this fact has deeply rooted that your worth is not like that to get the earning of 1 million per month or per day.

In your mental image, the people who are millionaires have qualities, according to you, they have a good appearance or good personality.

Believe me, money is an exchange of energy. Thinking negatively about money all the time will lead you towards a lack of money.

If you would understand this, giving money to someone will definitely create abundance in your life so you will not believe it but it's true because when you give money you add abundance to someone's life. You must be wondering. Why am I telling you all of sudden about money? Because for being a millionaire you first have to give your best to this nature which has infinite blessings for you even money also.

First, give yourself time and be the best version of your own. The beliefs that we had consisted for a long time, it's hard to disappear instantly. So, what best you can do is to give yourself a lot of time to understand better. In which we are good at it. How can you polish it? Or what else can you do? Rather than just making bread and butter for the family.

Multiple sources of income will lead you to be the best of your own.

Example: - If we make any sketch we try to give our best to make it perfect, hair to toe. So, why don't we do such hard work to be the one we want to be?

I am not asking you to work in many companies or work overtime.

I am asking you to work on yourself. Write down your quality on a piece of paper. "Don't say you don't have quality" if you feel like this then I suggest you to read the "Importance of yours" topic again in this book and then come forward to write down your qualities and weakness.

What do you have to do after, you must be wondering, so just write down how can you polish your quality to make it excellent according to you and then how can you work on your weakness to make it your strength.

Example: -

o   Quality

- I am good at making a sketch

- I will give my 15 minutes daily to make it excellent.

o   Weakness

- I am not good at maths

- I will give my extra 20 minutes every day except the time I usually study maths where I will work more on this subject and I will try to understand where I am stuck in.

If you would do it in every area of your life such as health, money, relationships and career so nobody would able to stop you, to be the best version of your own.

The real meaning of the best version of you is becoming the person whom you desire to have everything you dream for, trust me that's your best version and for being it you need to first make yourself the best internally.

Your thoughts would make a difference and soon you will be in your dream place, the place you always want to go. The real bliss in life is when you live the life of your dream.

Be the best version of your own in every possible way and give yourself time as much as you can so that you can understand where you can work on yourself.

Example: - Priyanka Chopra worked on herself so much. She tried her level best to find her true version and as you can see now how many titles she won, just because she gave herself time and never doubted herself that she will be able to do it or not, as a human we tend to doubt our skills such as while taking any initiative towards our dream we always think, will we able to do it or not?

But once you win over your doubt as Priyanka Chopra did, so you can too achieve so many milestones like her. Everyone is unique so rather than comparing yourself to people, work on yourself.

Note: - Your dreams want your presence. Give wings to your dream so that you can experience the most beautiful journey of your life as being the best version of you.